Mimi and Violet Try Something New

Written by
Lisa Menzel

Illustrated by
Taranggana

This book is dedicated to my family.

You all inspire, challenge and support me in ways

thought impossible.

Kids; remember Mum and Dad's message:

"You can do anything, all you need to do is try!"

One Sunday morning Mum and Dad decided to take their daughters Mimi and Violet to try an activity they had never done before... ice-skating!

"Yes!" shouted Violet with excitement.
"I don't want to go skating" whined Mimi and she began to cry.
"Come on Mimi, it will be lots of fun!" said Dad, trying to encourage Mimi to have a go.
Mum gave Mimi a big hug.
"You'll be OK Mimi, we'll be there with you", she said.

While driving in the car, Mimi was feeling worried. She thought to herself: I can't skate. I'm going to fall over. Everyone will laugh at me. Her chest was starting to hurt and her tummy felt like butterflies were flying around in it!
Mimi looked over at Violet and noticed a big smile on her face.

Violet was feeling happy and excited about trying something new.
She couldn't wait to get there.
"I haven't tried ice-skating but I think it's going to be fun!" Violet exclaimed.

They finally arrived. "I don't want to go... I don't want to skate today... I want to go home" cried Mimi.
Violet could see that her sister was sad and held her hand to show that she cared about her. "Come on we can do this together" Violet said to Mimi.
Besides Violet didn't want to go home, she wanted to try something she had never done before.

They all put on the ice-skates. Dad helped Violet to stand up and balance.

"These skates are heavy" said Violet.

"Woah!" Violet took one step, lost her balance and fell over.

"Ouch! that hurt" muttered Violet.

"Oops! Up you get" Dad helped Violet to stand up.

"I want to try that again" she said with a firm voice.

Violet was feeling nervous about falling over again but she was so determined to learn how to skate that she focused on getting her balance. Violet tried to skate again and slid one foot in front of the other.

This time she was skating. "Look at me, look at me!" she cried. PLUNK! Violet was so excited that she lost her concentration and her balance and fell on to her bottom. Everyone laughed. Dad helped her to get back on to her feet so that she could try again. Violet fell over a few more times but each time she just kept getting back up!

Mum asked Mimi if she wanted to have a go.

"No. I can't do it" mumbled Mimi.

"I want a cuddle." Mimi began to cry.

Mimi was worried about trying new things and didn't think she could do it.

"You can do this Mimi. All you need to do is try. You can do anything if you just give it a go" said Mum with a soft calm voice. Mimi looked at her sister and saw how much fun she was having even though she had fallen over a few times.

Violet could see that Mimi was sad and encouraged her to give it a try.

"Come on Mimi, come skate with me" shouted Violet.

"I'm scared I won't be able to do it" Mimi said to Mum.

Then Mum gave Mimi a big cuddle and whispered:
"I know it seems really scary to try something new.
All you need to do is say to yourself:
I CAN DO THIS!"
"OK Mum, I'll put the skates on" said Mimi.

Mum helped Mimi to put on her skates. "How do they feel?" asked Mum.
"Funny" replied Mimi with a smile on her face.
"Now let's try to stand up" Mum held Mimi's hand and helped her to get her balance.
"I'm a bit wobbly" laughed Mimi.
"Try sliding one foot forward then the other" suggested Mum.

Mimi held on to mum's hand as she started to skate, squeezed her fingers and held on tight. Her hand was sweaty and those butterflies were still flying around in her tummy.
Mimi felt so nervous about falling over so she thought about what her Mum had told her:
"I CAN DO THIS, I CAN DO THIS, I CAN DO THIS!" she thought.

Mimi wanted to go let go of Mum's hand. So she let go and...she was skating all by herself! Mimi wanted to go faster and catch up to Violet to show her that she could skate without Mum's help. Mimi was feeling much more relaxed and noticed that the butterflies in her tummy had gone away.

Now she was having lots of fun! "Look at me Violet! I'm skating! Wait for me!"
Violet stopped and waited for her sister.
"Wow Mimi, you're skating. Well done!" encouraged Violet.
Both Mimi and Violet were feeling very proud of themselves because they had a go at trying something new.

The two sisters were now holding hands and skating together.
"This is so much fun!" shouted Mimi.
"Great job girls!" Mum and Dad jumped with excitement.
"I knew you could do it. You can do anything" they said.
"All you need to do is try!"

Helpful information for Parents

This book is part of a series that helps families explore childhood social - emotional development. As children grow and develop they learn their social interaction and coping skills within the family unit before testing them in their wider network, such as with their friends at school. Therefore, it is important that as parents, we can provide good role modelling and guidance in a positive and safe environment so that children can assess for themselves how to behave appropriately and cope with life's challenges.

You can help your child by:

- Reading this book with your child to open-up conversations about **thoughts and feelings**. For example: "I'm scared I won't be able to do it" is a statement about *fear*. There may be hidden **meanings and feelings** behind what children say, so be attentive and curious.
- Use **art materials** or **play games** with your child to encourage *playfulness*. This will help your child to relax and have happy or neutral feelings. While the child is focusing on something else, it will help to open-up conversation and explore otherwise difficult topics.
- Being a **role-model** for positive behaviour change is essential. Children learn from their primary carers so be aware of your own social interaction and coping skills and how this might impact and affect your child.
- **Acknowledge and praise** your child when they have demonstrated positive approaches to challenges. This is the most effective way children learn. Also, **acknowledge, praise and foster your child's strengths** as this will help to build their **self-esteem**.
- Seek **professional counselling** if you need further strategies, support and assistance. There are effective evidence-based therapeutic approaches that can help your family.

We all experience stress and anxiety at times in life and in different ways. **Anxiety is a normal feeling** like feeling happy or sad. We need normal levels of stress and anxiety to help us to be motivated to complete tasks but when there are high and prolonged levels of stress, worry and anxiety, this can impact our daily functioning and become a problem. There are different types of anxiety and children can have various reactions or demonstrate various behaviours in response to their worries, stress or fears. Therefore, it is important to understand your own child's coping strategies and assess the severity of the reaction and impact it might be causing. Teach and guide your child to be **resilient** – a skill that will help them flourish in becoming confident and competent human beings with a strong sense of wellbeing.
Try not to feel stressed, pressured or demoralised if you don't get it right all the time. There is no such thing as a 'perfect parent'! Be encouraged to try again with a new or different approach and this will demonstrate to your child that parents can make mistakes too and that's OK, as long as we are all learning along the way.

For more information or to contact the Author visit:

wellwithincounselling.com.au